Living Room in Africa

by Bathsheba Doran

SAMUEL FRENCH

FOUNDED 1830

NEW YORK HOLLYWOOD LONDON TORONTO

SAMUELFRENCH.COM

ISBN 978-0-573-66345-1   Printed in U.S.A.   #13763

IMPORTANT BILLING AND CREDIT REQUIREMENTS

All producers of *LIVING ROOM IN AFRICA must* give credit to the Author of the Play in all programs distributed in connection with performances of the Play, and in all instances in which the title of the Play appears for the purposes of advertising, publicizing or otherwise exploiting the Play and/or a production. The name of the Author *must* appear on a separate line on which no other name appears, immediately following the title and *must* appear in size of type not less than fifty percent of the size of the title type.

In addition the following credit *must* be given in all programs and publicity information distributed in association with this piece:

The Edge Theatre Company (NYC) March 13th – April 15th 2006
Directed by Carolyn Cantor
World Premiere, The Beckett Theatre @ Theatre Row

LIVING ROOM IN AFRICA was produced by Gloucester Stage Company at Gloucester Stage in 2005. Production information is as follows:

MARIE . . . . Polly Lee
NSUGO . . . . Jackie Davis
MARK . . . . Richard Arum
EDWARD . . . . Nathaniel McIntyre
ANTHONY . . . . Billy Eugene Jones
MICHAEL LEE . . . . Sean McGuirk

Set Design . . . . Jenna McFarland
Costume Design . . . . Kristen Glans
Lighting Design . . . . Scott Pinkney
Sound Design . . . . Matt Griffin
Production Stage Manager . . . . Adele Nadine Traub
Directed by . . . . Danny Goldstein

LIVING ROOM IN AFRICA was produced Off-Broadway by Edge Theater at The Beckett Theater at Theater Row in 2006. Production information is as follows:

MARIE . . . . Ana Reeder
NSUGO . . . . Marsha Stephanie Blake
MARK . . . . Michael Chernus
EDWARD . . . . Rob Campbell
ANTHONY . . . . Maduka Steady
MICHAEL LEE . . . . Guy Boyd

Set Design . . . . David Korins
Costume Design . . . . Jenny Mannis
Lighting Design . . . . Matt Richards
Sound . . . . Eric Shim
Original Music . . . . Michael Friedman
Production Stage Manager . . . . Jeff Meyers
Directed by . . . . Carolyn Cantor

CHARACTERS

Marie – late twenties/early thirties
Edward – late twenties/early thirties
Mark – mid twenties
Anthony – mid twenties
Nsugo – late twenties/early thirties
Michael Lee – early sixties

"When tremendous changes are involved no one can be blamed for looking to his own intent. We consider that we are worthy of our power."
Thucydides, *A History of the Peloponnesian War*

"The key-note is to be: the prolific growth of our intellectual life, in literature, art, etc – and in contrast to this: the whole of mankind has gone astray."
Ibsen, *Notes and Fragments*

"They stumble all night over bones of the dead:
And feel they know not what but care;
And wish to lead others when they should be lead."
William Blake, *The Voice of the Ancient Bard*

For Lucy

ACT I

(A living room in Africa. Boxes waiting to be unpacked. We're in a large, somewhat dilapidated house. On one wall, a faint outline where a zebra skin used to hang. Various pieces of contemporary Western art leaning against the walls, incongruous in their surroundings. A winding staircase leads to a second floor. The room is still for a moment. **MARK** *and* **MARIE** *enter.)*

MARIE. Do you like the house?

MARK. Yes it's very... lots of wicker.

MARIE. I like it. The city, where the gallery is going to be, that's about an hour's drive away. We'll go there for dinner, I thought. Maybe tomorrow. And Edward will want to show you the site and everything.

MARK. The city's an hour's drive?

MARIE. Yes, but there's a local village. That's only about a twenty-minute walk.

MARK. What do you do there?

MARIE. It's a sort of... a permanent market. You can get a cup of coffee. And now there's a swimming pool.

MARK. They have a pool?

MARIE. As of today. Edward had it built. Or dug, I suppose. For the local children.

MARK. What's wrong with the river?

MARIE. Mark!

MARK. What? I thought everybody swam in the river.

MARIE. They do. It's polluted. Hence the swimming pool.

MARK. Polluted with what?

MARIE. A disease.

MARK. Polluted is from something unnatural. Like traffic.

MARIE. It's something to do with rats.

MARK. Weil's disease. It's a parasite.

MARIE. I don't know. It's very dangerous. We have been informed by everyone not to swim in the river. But the children still swim in it. Or some of them do. Because they won't listen. Edward thought a pool would distract them. Although of course it can't fit as many of them in.

MARK. They have the same problem in England. Remember the summer Mum and Dad wouldn't let us swim in the river in Oxford?

MARIE. Oh yes. Well it's that then. Here.

MARK. So where's Edward?

MARIE. At the swimming pool. Today is the opening ceremony. He's giving a speech. They're naming it after him. The Edward Lawrence Swimming pool.

MARK. He didn't want to put your name on it?

MARIE. We're not married.

(A beat.)

MARK. Could I have a drink?

MARIE. Oh. Oh I'm sorry. What would you like?

MARK. Do you have any beer?

MARIE. We have gin. Edward thought it would be appropriate to drink gin in Africa. Like the colonialists of old.

(She makes him a gin and tonic. Everything she needs is on a subtle and convenient drinks trolley, including ice.)

MARIE. *(cont'd)* I can't believe you're here.

MARK. I can't believe you're here.

MARIE. I know. It's so far away.

(She hands him his drink, and he takes a long sip.)

MARK. That's good.

MARIE. Is it? Good. Edward's got in the habit of having one every evening when he gets home from work.

MARK. It's really hot.

MARIE. So, how are you? Is everything well?

MARK. Yes. Yes, everything's… well. How are you?

MARIE. I'm happy.

MARK. Good. You look well.

MARIE. I am. I really… Mark, I really think I've found my rhythm. And it's much slower than I thought it was.

MARK. Well it couldn't have been faster.

MARIE. You should try one of these.

(She hands him a red reed, from a neat wooden box.)

The natives chew them. Local culture.

(She laughs slightly.)

I'll go and stir the soup. It's cold soup you'll be relieved to know. Of mango.

(She exits.)

MARK. You're cooking?

(MARK laughs slightly, then stands up and walks around the room a little. He picks up a few pieces of African bric-a-brac.

Outside, there is a scream. Then some voices speaking, indistinguishable. Then nothing.)

MARK. *(cont'd)* Marie?

(A young black woman enters from upstairs of the house.)

Hello. Hi.

(She walks straight past MARK and into another room. A moment later MARIE comes back in.)

Who was that woman?

MARIE. That? That was Nsugo.

MARK. And she is… ?

MARIE. She helps.

MARK. She's the help?

MARIE. Yes, she's the help.

MARK. You've enslaved the natives?

MARIE. *(Sharply)* She's not a slave, Mark, is she? She's being paid. A lot.

MARK. How much?

MARIE. I'm not telling you.

MARK. *(winding her up)* Just tell me how much.

MARIE. She came with the house. *(A beat.)* It's just because she's black. Everyone's black here. What am I supposed to do? *(A beat.)* And Edward wanted it. Alright? I hate it. *(A beat.)* She's teaching me to cook, actually.

MARK. Since when have you been interested in cooking?

MARIE. Since now. I told you. I'm changing. So how is everyone?

MARK. Fine. I bumped into your friend Pete. He said to tell you 'hello.'

MARIE. Is that it?

MARK. Yes.

MARIE. Well say 'hello' back, I suppose. Or not. I don't know. If Marie says 'hello' in Africa, does anybody hear?

MARK. He read one of your poems in the paper.

MARIE. Which poem?

MARK. In *The Times.*

MARIE. Oh that. That was a while ago.

MARK. What are you working on now?

MARIE. I don't really want to talk about work.

MARK. Alright.

MARIE. I'll take you on a tour tomorrow. It's unbelievable.

MARK. What is?

MARIE. The poverty.

MARK. Not much point in showing it to me then, is there? If it's unbelievable.

MARIE. No. I suppose not. *(A beat.)* There's lots of other things to do.

MARK. Like what?

MARIE. You can hand feed giraffes, about half an hour from here. I thought we'd do that. And there's a place to watch… hippos bathe. I thought we could do that. And there's a lake a couple of hours away. I can't remember what it's called, but it's supposed to be beautiful. There are… flamingoes.

MARK. That sounds good. The flamingoes. *(A beat.)* You should call Pete.

MARIE. Why?

MARK. Because he used to be a friend of yours. I don't think you should cut yourself off so much.

MARIE. The phone's expensive.

MARK. Can't Edward pay?

MARIE. I like to keep things separate.

MARK. You really chew that stuff? Often?

MARIE. Yes, why?

MARK. Your teeth have gone slightly red.

MARIE. Really? Have they? I'll have to clean them. Are you tired? You must be tired.

MARK. No. I feel slightly dirty. I think I should wash.

MARIE. There's a shower upstairs. They put it in specially.

MARK. Congratulations.

MARIE. Thanks, I feel good about it. Edward wants to try and install air conditioning although I don't think the wiring here can take it. Actually I don't know anything about it but nobody else thinks the wiring here can take it. There'd be a fire.

MARK. Are you planning to do a lot of home improvements?

MARIE. Obviously, I'm not. Edward is. He's going to be investigating air-conditioning. I'm supposed to be sourcing rugs.

MARK. How long do you think you'll be staying? About?

MARIE. I don't know. A year, two years. About. I do like it here. I'll still be coming back to visit. Just like I did from New York. And Germany.

MARK. This is a lot more inconvenient than flying to New York. Also…

MARIE. Also what?

MARK. I'm getting married.

(A beat.)

MARIE. To who?

MARK. To a girl.

MARIE. Oh.

MARK. You haven't met her.

MARIE. What's her name?

MARK. It's Lilly.

MARIE. That's wonderful. When did you meet her?

MARK. I've been with her for about eight months.

MARIE. Quick.

MARK. I… really… It turns out, you just know. When you've met the right person. I've wasted rather a lot of time.

MARIE. You've never mentioned her.

MARK. I have, actually. I really want you to meet her.

MARIE. I will meet her.

MARK. When?

MARIE. At Christmas.

MARK. Oh come on, I'm getting married. I'm getting married!

MARIE. I've only been here a month… I can't just fly back because you want me to meet your girlfriend. Your fiancée.

MARK. Why not?

MARIE. You want me to fly back for dinner?

MARK. I just flew here.

MARIE. Do you know, I think we've got some champagne? Edward actually brought it over from New York. He's so strange. He brought some champagne, and all the tea we had. Isn't that strange?

(A beat.)

Mark… Don't be angry. We'll both fly over for the wedding. Of course. I can't wait to meet her. What's she like? *(A beat.)* This is wonderful… What colour hair does she have?

MARK. Blonde. It's blonde.

MARIE. What does she do?

MARK. She's a doctor. *(A beat.)* Mum and Dad love her.

MARIE. Why didn't you introduce me to her last time I was in London?

MARK. She was away that weekend.

MARIE. It wasn't a weekend.

MARK. I'm going to have children.

MARIE. Really? How many?

MARK. Four. I've decided. You're not going to know them.

MARIE. I will know them. I can visit. And they can visit. Imagine what a wonderful time they'd have here. Imagine the photographs. They could ride elephants.

MARK. No one is going to visit you here.

MARIE. What do you mean no one is gong to visit me here?

MARK. This country is dying, isn't it? I'm sure anyone who can is trying to move away.

MARIE. Not everyone's dead.

MARK. You're not really staying here…

MARIE. I'm writing.

MARK. You could write in England.

MARIE. I don't want to live in London again.

MARK. Mum and Dad said you turned down a teaching fellowship there.

MARIE. Edward got this opportunity.

MARK. What about your career?

MARIE. Poets don't have careers.

MARK. The best career a poet can hope for is to teach.

(*A beat.*)

MARIE. I do have a life, Mark. I'm sorry if you don't like it, but I'm not planning to change it. For you.

MARK. Because of Edward?

MARIE. Partly.

MARK. It's ridiculous.

MARIE. What is?

MARK. You just showed me the house, you sleep in separate bedrooms!

MARIE. Not everyone wants what you want, Mark.

MARK. I assumed… We all assumed that you two must be… by now…

MARIE. Well we're not.

MARK. Why?

MARIE. Because we're friends! Old, old friends! It may not be the way everyone else is, but I'm not the way everyone else is. You may not like it here but I do.

MARK. Really? In this god-forsaken village.

MARIE. It's not forsaken.

MARK. There's nothing here!

MARIE. They think the gallery is going to make a big difference.

MARK. Only to people looking for an interesting article in the Sunday papers.

MARIE. To the whole area. A lot of people are getting work through it.

MARK. Edward! And I'd love to know how much he's being paid. Not that he even needs paying. How much did he make from selling that last piece?

MARIE. He's in charge of about twenty men, actually. He's overseeing the construction. They are all being paid. Anyway, what have you suddenly got against Edward?

MARK. I don't think he… I don't think he takes care of you.

MARIE. He does, Mark. Oh, he does. We both take care of each other.

MARK. Don't you want to be with someone who…

MARIE. I can bear Edward. I can't bear most people.

(A beat.)

MARK. Alright. I'll take that shower.

MARIE. You're not angry are you?

MARK. No.

MARIE. Good. Because you just got here.

*(**MARK** exits. **MARIE** makes herself a drink. **NSUGO** enters with plates.)*

MARIE. *(cont'd)* We already had a fight.

Will you taste the soup?

NSUGO. Yes.

(NSUGO exits with the plates into the dining room.)

MARIE. I think it's good. Tomorrow I'll try and make it without you helping. Then you can taste it and give me a mark out of ten.

(NSUGO reenters, and straightens up the room.)

NSUGO. Alright.

MARIE. We're still going to have our cooking lessons while Mark's here. He can amuse himself for an hour. And I'm still going to write. I don't have to stop everything just because he's arrived, do I? Or do I?

NSUGO. He is coming a long way to see you.

MARIE. Yes. But I can't spend every second with him because I'll kill him by the middle of the week. That's how it is with brothers, isn't it? You love them so much in theory. Do you have a brother?

NSUGO. One brother.

MARIE. Does he live around here?

NSUGO. He is living in Ghana. It is expensive to go there.

MARIE. Yes. Do you get along well?

NSUGO. I do not know my brother so much now. He is married in Ghana. I do not know the wife.

MARIE. My brother is getting married too.

(NSUGO is about to exit.)

Nsugo? How do you manage it all? Michael Lee told us you have four children. Would you like to bring them here, sometimes? So you can be near them? How old are they?

NSUGO. One is eight and one is nine.

MARIE. What about the others?

NSUGO. The others are dead now.

MARIE. What? What did they die of?

NSUGO. There is sickness.

MARIE. Yes. *(A beat.)* Are you well?

NSUGO. I am well.

MARIE. Good.

(EDWARD enters.)

EDWARD. Hello!

NSUGO. I can finish with the table.

(She exits.)

EDWARD. How was your day?

MARIE. I wrote. There's a place in the village. I got a lot of stares.

EDWARD. What place?

MARIE. With the wooden tables. It looks rather like a shack.

EDWARD. Oh there. It is a shack.

MARIE. It's a café. And they're very nice. I had papaya juice and coffee. And a chapatti.

(EDWARD makes himself a gin.)

EDWARD. What's the coffee like?

MARIE. Strong.

EDWARD. When are you going to show me what you're working on?

MARIE. Not yet.

EDWARD. Do you want to talk it through?

MARIE. No.

EDWARD. So where's Mark?

MARIE. Upstairs. Showering.

EDWARD. How is it seeing him?

MARIE. He wants me to go home.

EDWARD. He always says that. He misses you. This tonic is rather flat.

MARIE. And he thinks it's odd that we have a black cook.

EDWARD. I know, but what are we supposed to do? Everyone here's black.

MARIE. I know.

EDWARD. She needs the money. It's a good thing. We don't need her. I miss cooking.

MARIE. I know.

EDWARD. I mean it. We come here, we've got all of this money as far as they're concerned, she asks us for a job, she used to work here… I mean for God's sake, what were we supposed to do? She's got four children.

MARIE. Two.

EDWARD. No, four.

MARIE. No, when Michael Lee was here she had four children. Now she has two. She just told me.

(A beat.)

EDWARD. What did they die of?

MARIE. She wasn't specific.

EDWARD. We should find out.

MARIE. Why?

EDWARD. Well because… We ought to know.

MARIE. She's fine. I asked.

EDWARD. I'm worried now.

Do you think we should ask her to get a doctor's certificate?

MARIE. No, I don't.

EDWARD. What should we do?

MARIE. She said she's fine.

EDWARD. Because she needs this job.

MARIE. Yes, she does. What would happen if we gave her whatever you'd pay a maid in New York? She'd be able to up and go to Spain after a couple of weeks. Get a nice suntan. *(A beat.)* Sorry. I don't know why I said that.

EDWARD. Tomorrow I thought we could eat at that place that's started up by the gallery. You see? It's already happening. Regeneration. Before we've even opened.

MARIE. Alright. And I thought we might hand feed giraffes.

EDWARD. How many times have we handfed giraffes since we moved here?

MARIE. Three.

EDWARD. Right.

MARIE. And their tongues are grey.

EDWARD. Very powerful hearts giraffes. Got to keep the blood pumping all the way up that great long neck.

MARIE. They are such an extraordinary shape. I think of them as the animal equivalent to bananas. Can we have a dinner party while Mark's here?

EDWARD. Who would we invite?

MARIE. There's the people from the gallery.

EDWARD. Who? The builders? I don't think that would be…

MARIE. When does everyone else arrive?

EDWARD. In a couple of months when we're ready to open.

MARIE. What about that guy you told me about? Anthony.

EDWARD. Oh him. The contractor. We could have him, I suppose. That would be nice. Who's going to cook?

MARIE. You cook. You never cook any more.

EDWARD. It'll look odd. I don't think any of the men Anthony knows cook.

MARIE. What do they do, beat their wives? You can enlighten him.

EDWARD. What would I cook?

MARIE. Chicken and potatoes, please.

EDWARD. Would I cook it African style or Western?

MARIE. Can you cook it African style?

EDWARD. Sort of.

MARIE. Can you cook it African style as good as Anthony's wife? Wives.

EDWARD. Probably not.

MARIE. Then Western.

EDWARD. When?

MARIE. At the end of the week. It can be Mark's goodbye.

EDWARD. I can't believe he flew all the way to see us already. Well, to see you.

MARIE. I know. The idea of getting in a plane fills me with dread.

EDWARD. It's a shorter flight from London than we had from New York.

MARIE. Really? Maybe that's where I'll go next.

EDWARD. I thought you were spending Christmas in New York.

MARIE. Mark's getting married.

EDWARD. Really? To what?

MARIE. To Lilly, whoever she is. Lilly the fucking doctor.

EDWARD. We should open some champagne for him. Make a special event out of it. We'll still have another bottle.

(MARK enters.)

MARK. Good shower.

MARIE. Thanks.

EDWARD. Hello!

MARK. Hi.

(MARK and EDWARD hug.)

EDWARD. So you got here okay. Obviously.

MARIE. He took the bus.

MARK. Two busses.

EDWARD. Really? That's very enterprising of you. Everyone normally takes a cab.

MARIE. Except the people on the bus.

EDWARD. Except the people on the bus. Indeed.
I hear you're getting married.

MARK. Yes.

EDWARD. So who is she?

MARK. To Lilly. She's a doctor.

MARIE. She has blonde hair.

EDWARD. I think we've got a bottle of champagne some-where.

(He exits.)

MARIE. Mark. I am very, very happy for you.

(Hugging him)

I can't wait to meet Lilly.

MARK. She's nervous to meet you.

MARIE. Good.

*(**EDWARD** comes back in with the champagne, and champagne glasses. He hands the others their glasses and then pops opens the bottle. He pours them their drinks.)*

EDWARD. I told you we should bring the champagne.

MARIE. Yes, it's wonderful isn't it, with champagne? You have a bottle, and you never know what the occasion will be to use it, but one always comes along and here it is.

EDWARD. When's the wedding?

MARK. Next spring.

EDWARD. We'll be there!

So what's she like?

MARK. Her name's Lilly. She's a doctor.

EDWARD. Lilly's a beautiful name. I always wanted to name a daughter Lilly.

MARK. *(sarcastically)* You two thinking about having kids?

MARIE. Did you see the soup? I helped to make it.

EDWARD. Oh that was you. Very impressive. I just added some salt.

MARIE. Why would you add salt to a mango? That makes no sense.

EDWARD. So that it isn't too sweet? So that it has taste?

MARIE. The taste of salt.

MARK. I hear you built the villagers a swimming pool.

*(**NSUGO** enters.)*

NSUGO. The table is ready.

(She exits.)

EDWARD. I'm going to have to talk to her about this. I don't feel comfortable.

MARIE. What exactly are you going to say?

MARK. What's the problem?

MARIE. Edward thinks the cook may have AIDS.

EDWARD. I'm worried. She's doing the cooking. What if she cuts her finger or something?

MARIE. You don't have to eat the food she has prepared if you don't want to. I will.

EDWARD. Mark…

MARIE. The cook here may or may not have AIDS. She says she doesn't. Anyway, you don't get it from eating food.

EDWARD. You're being deliberately perverse.

MARK. You don't get it from food.

MARIE. She's not going to give us food with her blood in it. Is she? Shall we go through?

(Outside, a scream.)

MARK. What is that?

EDWARD. We don't know. It's rather worrying.

MARK. Yes it is. Do you ever go and see who it is?

MARIE. People scream everywhere. They screamed in New York. They screamed in Germany. Don't you ever hear people screaming in London?

MARK. I suppose so.

MARIE. And I doubt you go outside to deal with it.

EDWARD. You can't go out and investigate at night. The animals.

MARK. Really?

EDWARD. You can actually be eaten by a lion here. We were warned.

MARK. Do you have a gun?

EDWARD. Yes we do, we have a gun. Although I have no idea how to shoot it. Or any intention of learning.

MARIE. We're thinking, if a lion sees the gun, that will be enough.

MARK. I don't think that's how it works with lions.

MARIE. No. Me neither. Shall we go through?

(Exit.)

ACT II

(It is seven o'clock in the evening, a week later. The house is mostly unpacked. **MARK** *and* **ANTHONY** *are seated, with drinks nearby. Anthony is showing Mark some photographs.*

ANTHONY. That is the supermarket I built in the city. It took nearly a year. Everybody there uses it now. That was my biggest job. That is what got me the job to build the gallery. This is the swimming pool.

MARK. Edward's swimming pool?

ANTHONY. Yes. Yes. But they drained it. We have to refill it. And this is the gallery. How it is at the moment. It will not be finished for another two or three months, but you can see here... this is the front. This will all be glass. That is my friend, Nick. He is working on the roof, you see? And that's me, see? I am telling everyone where the door will go. My friend took that picture. Not Nick. My other friend. He is also working on the building. He is a plumber.

*(**MARIE** enters hurriedly.)*

MARIE. Edward!

(To the others)

I'll be with you in a minute.

(She stops and smiles at them.)

Are you alright for drinks?

MARK. Yes.

MARIE. Edward! The rice...

(She turns back to the others, laughing slightly)

I've burned the rice.

ANTHONY. Where is Nsugo?

25

MARIE. She… We had to… You see her children are sick. Her other children. She's taking care of them.

ANTHONY. Oh.

MARIE. We…

MARK. Weren't you looking for Edward?

MARIE. Yes. Thank you.

(**MARIE** *exits upstairs.* **MARK** *tries to hand the photographs back to Anthony.*)

MARK. Good work.

ANTHONY. Keep them.

MARK. No, that's alright.

ANTHONY. No, you show them to people. Maybe they'll want me to build something. In England.

MARK. I'm afraid I don't know anyone that –

ANTHONY. Just in case. I have many copies. And then you will have a picture of me. One day you will look at it and say "that was Anthony."

(**MARK** *takes the photographs and puts them down.*)

You have been here for a week. What do you think of my country?

MARK. I like it. It's very beautiful.

ANTHONY. Yes, it's beautiful. The women are beautiful, right?

MARK. Yes.

ANTHONY. You like them, huh? I could find you a woman if you want. There are many women you could see.

MARK. Many thanks but I'm leaving tomorrow.

ANTHONY. Yes. You are leaving. I want to leave. Maybe go to America. Edward knows a lot of people in America. He could get me a visa. I could build things there. Maybe swimming pools. Everyone has a swimming pool in California, right?

MARK. I don't know. I think a lot of people do.

ANTHONY. Edward knows a lot of rich people, right?

MARK. Some.

ANTHONY. He has a lot of money. The other man who came, Michael Lee, he was going to get me a job. But so far nothing. You've been to America?

MARK. Yes.

ANTHONY. Do you like it there?

MARK. Not really. I prefer England.

ANTHONY. Where do you live in England?

MARK. London.

ANTHONY. Oh, London! What do you do there?

MARK. I research. Energy. Different types of energy. What the best way for us to make power is.

ANTHONY. Here we use coal.

MARK. I know.

ANTHONY. Is that one of the best ones?

MARK. There are advantages and disadvantages.

ANTHONY. Same with everything. If I leave here I won't see the mountains but I will make a lot of money, maybe.

(MARIE *enters hurriedly.*)

MARIE. Edward's in the shower. Mark, can you look at the rice? It's not…

MARK. What's wrong with it?

MARIE. I don't know, can you just fix it?

(MARK *exits.*)

Thank you.

(*To* ANTHONY)

Can I get you another gin? Oh you're still drinking. Alright. I'll have one.

(MARIE *gets herself a drink.*)

Edward says you're doing wonderful work at the gallery.

ANTHONY. He likes me, yes?

MARIE. Oh yes.

ANTHONY. I am not lazy. I make sure everything gets done.

MARIE. That's good.

ANTHONY. The workers, they want to take a long time. I crack the whip.

MARIE. Why do they want to take such a long time?

ANTHONY. There is no other work after this job. Not for them.

MARIE. You know some very rich men have put their money in this project. So if the men want to take a little bit longer I think that's okay. They hope the gallery will create jobs.

ANTHONY. Only three or four. And not for these men.

(MARK comes back in.)

MARK. I've put more rice on.

MARIE. *(To ANTHONY)* Do you like rice?

ANTHONY. Sure, rice. Rice is very popular.

(EDWARD comes in.)

EDWARD. Hello. Hello, Anthony.

ANTHONY. Hey Edward!

(They slap each other's palms.)

MARIE. Darling, there was a problem with the rice which I have solved.

EDWARD. What problem?

MARIE. I burnt it. Mark's put more on. Thank you, Mark.

(To EDWARD)

But I think you should turn down the chicken.

EDWARD. How does she burn rice?

MARK. She didn't put enough water in.

(EDWARD and ANTHONY laugh. MARK leaves the group to browse the bookshelves.)

ANTHONY. *(to MARIE)* You can't cook. Wow!

MARIE. Edward does the cooking.

(To EDWARD)

Are you going to turn down the chicken?

EDWARD. *(Sharply)* In a minute.

MARIE. Can you cook, Anthony?

ANTHONY. No.

MARIE. That's something we have in common then.

EDWARD. Who wants some more?

(ANTHONY *holds out his glass.*)

Are there any local wines here we should try?

(MARK *holds out his glass as well, and* EDWARD *crosses to serve him.*)

ANTHONY. I don't know.

MARIE. What do people drink?

ANTHONY. Beer. Or there is a spirit called Khadi. That's good. Made from berries.

EDWARD. We should get some. Where do you get it?

ANTHONY. At the store.

(*A beat.*)

MARIE. Do you want some Khat?

(*She shows Anthony the red reeds.*)

ANTHONY. No. I don't chew it.

MARIE. Oh. Why don't you?

ANTHONY. It's not good for you. Some people, friends of mine, they chew Khat all day, every day, they don't do anything anymore. I have chewed it sometimes. It can make you see things.

MARK. Is it hallucinogenic?

EDWARD. Slightly. I'll turn down the chicken.

(EDWARD *exits.*)

MARIE. Have you always lived here?

ANTHONY. Yes.

MARIE. Are you married?

ANTHONY. Yes. I am.

MARIE. Do you have children?

ANTHONY. One.

MARIE. Boy or a girl?

ANTHONY. A girl. She is one.

MARIE. I wish you had brought your wife.

ANTHONY. She is with the baby.

MARIE. I like babies. You could have brought them. Next time.

ANTHONY. Edward and I must talk about work.

MARIE. I could have talked to your wife.

ANTHONY. She does not have much English.

    *(***EDWARD** *comes back in.)*

MARIE. I was telling Anthony, next time he should bring his wife.

EDWARD. Anthony, I didn't know you were married.

ANTHONY. I am married. One year.

MARIE. He has a baby.

EDWARD. Why didn't you tell me?

    *(***ANTHONY** *shrugs.)*

    You should have brought them with you. We'd love to meet them.

ANTHONY. You two. You will have children soon?

MARIE. I don't know about soon. Mark's getting married next year.

ANTHONY. So Edward. We have a problem with the swimming pool.

EDWARD. What problem?

ANTHONY. It has been drained.

EDWARD. Oh why on earth have they done that?

ANTHONY. There was some blood in the water. A child hurt his head.

EDWARD. So they drained it? That seems a bit excessive.

ANTHONY. In the river, the water runs. In the pool the blood floats. There were other children in the pool so –. There was a lot of blood. People swallowed the water.

MARK. The child who hurt his head. He's alright, is he?

ANTHONY. Yes. But some people do not want to put more water in the pool. You have to talk to them.

EDWARD. Oh dear. Do you think I should send the family some flowers?

MARIE. It's not your fault.

EDWARD. I know, but it's my swimming pool.

(*to* **ANTHONY**)

Why don't they want to refill it?

ANTHONY. Some say the child was sick. He should not have been in the swimming pool. He was supposed to be separate. You should not send his mother anything.

MARIE. Sick with what?

ANTHONY. I don't know.

(*To* **EDWARD**)

You must get me the job to fill it. It will be a day's work. I need two men.

EDWARD. You shouldn't only stand and watch, Anthony. I did hire you to work as well.

ANTHONY. Okay. One man. I'll take Nick.

EDWARD. I'll talk to them tomorrow.

MARK. What's the child sick with? Is it AIDS?

ANTHONY. I don't know. Maybe. Some say.

MARK. How many others were in the pool?

ANTHONY. It was full.

EDWARD. There couldn't have been that much blood.

ANTHONY. There was a lot of blood.

MARK. Is someone checking the other children?

ANTHONY. No one is checking the other children. It is fine.

MARK. It's not fine. The other children should be seen by a doctor. This child should be seen by a doctor.

ANTHONY. This child was seen by a doctor!

MARK. Edward, I think you should arrange for a medical check.

EDWARD. Mark, there are medical facilities. I do not control the use people make of them.

(*A beat.*)

ANTHONY. This disease is very dangerous. You all have to be careful. It is very contagious. You can catch it from cups and plates and sometimes clothes. You have to stay separate. Remember, Edward? How I make sure you have a special cup in the gallery? That is why.

MARK. That's not how you catch it.

ANTHONY. What do you know?

MARK. I know you don't catch it from cups. You catch it from blood.

ANTHONY. It is in the air.

EDWARD. I know it feels that way, Anthony. But it's not. There has been a lot of research about it. In the West.

ANTHONY. How do you get it?

EDWARD. *(Uncomfortably)* Through sex. Mainly.

ANTHONY. No.

MARK. Yes!

ANTHONY. Then why do the children have it?

EDWARD. If the mother has it...

ANTHONY. Oh the mother... Yes.

MARIE. That's why you have to use a condom. Anthony. You must tell everyone to use a condom.

(*To* **MARK**)

That's one of the problems here.

EDWARD. *(To* **MARK***)* Condoms aren't actually that easy to get over here. We brought a few hundred with us from New York, but we're not quite sure what to do with them.

MARK. I'm sure.

ANTHONY. Many people think that condoms can give you AIDS.

MARK. What?

ANTHONY. But you say it is to protect you from the mother.

EDWARD. No –

MARK. Hey! Condoms do not give you AIDS. Spread the word.

ANTHONY. Alright. Relax man. Relax Max...

MARK. *(to* **ANTHONY***)* Why are you laughing? It's not funny. This is serious!

ANTHONY. *(sharply)* Not for you.

(*A beat.*)

MARIE. Why do people think it's happening?

ANTHONY. I don't know. Some people say from God. Maybe the men get it from the women. Like Edward said.

EDWARD. I did not say that. Please don't tell people that, Anthony.

MARK. Hey! Anthony! Where do you think the women get it from?

ANTHONY. Maybe a punishment. I don't know. Only God knows. It has happened before.

MARIE. When has it happened before?

ANTHONY. Fever. Sickness. No food, sometimes. Everywhere. It is part of living in Africa. That's why I want to move to America.

MARK. It's in America too. Did you know that? It's everywhere!

MARIE. There's medicine in America.

ANTHONY. I did not know that. Why don't they bring it here?

(*A beat.*)

EDWARD. It's too expensive.

MARIE. At the moment.

ANTHONY. The people who are sick in America. Why do they have it? Is it a punishment?

EDWARD. No. It's a disease. It's no one's fault.

ANTHONY. When the white man first came to this country, he got sick and died from fever. Because the land was not his to take. Now, here in Africa we get sick and die. Because we have done nothing with the land since the white man left. Why not? Why is this country not like America? There are rivers, there are trees, there are men to build. But there is no energy. There is a punishment for this I think.

EDWARD. I think the food's ready.

MARK. It's no one's fault.

ANTHONY. And yes, a woman gets it if she has been whoring. Everyone knows. The mother of this child today, she sees many men.

MARK. My god…

MARIE. Mark –

MARK. I'm going for a walk.

MARIE. Mark, stay.

MARK. *(To **ANTHONY**)* Whores don't get it! People get it! And it's not their fault!

(Exiting)

I don't want any dinner. Sorry.

MARIE. Mark. Please. We're not supposed to go out at night.

MARK. *(To **ANTHONY**, from the door)* You get it from sex. Use a condom.

MARIE. Mark, he's married.

ANTHONY. Hey, Mark! I am a Christian. That is why I don't use a condom.

MARK. Oh because you're a Christian?

ANTHONY. Just like you.

*(A beat. **MARK** exits.)*

Hey! What's his problem?

EDWARD. I'm so sorry.

MARIE. Edward –

EDWARD. What do you want me to do?

MARIE. He's upset. He's leaving tomorrow. He can't leave like this.

EDWARD. He'll be back in five minutes. He doesn't know where to go. There is nowhere to go.

MARIE. I'll get him. He's probably just waiting outside.

ANTHONY. I will leave.

MARIE. No. Let's sort this out. Mark didn't mean... He's concerned. He's concerned for your people.

ANTHONY. My people are not his concern.

MARIE. I'll go and get him. Please. Let's not. Let's not be this way. We are four people. In a room.

(She exits.)

EDWARD. Two people.

ANTHONY. I won't stay.

EDWARD. Are you sure? I am so sorry about Mark. They're both very highly strung.

ANTHONY. You have to look after everyone, yes? It is tiring. I get tired. That is why, you and me at work. In the sun. Shirts off. Only time a man can think, yes?

EDWARD. Why didn't you tell me you were married, Anthony? Anthony?

ANTHONY. I can not take my wife to America.

EDWARD. Why not?

ANTHONY. It's too much trouble. It's ok. I have a brother in Tanzania who sends his wife money. I will send my wife money.

EDWARD. Wouldn't you miss her? What about the baby?

ANTHONY. When are you going away?

EDWARD. After the gallery is established.

ANTHONY. I could go with you. I could be your assistant. I think you like having me around. I think I make you laugh.

EDWARD. I don't think you should leave your wife and child, Anthony. I don't want to play any part in that.

ANTHONY. I am a good builder, Edward. You are not a good builder. If I had not pushed you that wall would have come down on your head, remember?

EDWARD. Yes.

ANTHONY. I saved your life. Do you remember? I said now we are brothers.

*(**EDWARD** starts for the door.)*

EDWARD. Let's go. I should find Mark and Marie. They shouldn't be out there.

*(**ANTHONY** does not move.)*

ANTHONY. Do not leave me like Michael Lee left me, Edward. He promised me many things. I have been to this house many times before and the last time I left it he said "see you in America." And since then I have received one T-Shirt in the mail with one postcard with a picture of some boats on it. We are good friends, you and I. We have become friends. We work together, like men, every day under the sun, sweating and building. You make promises. You must not betray me. It is easy to get on a plane and fly away.

(He starts to exit and then turns back.)

My wife is sick, Edward. She is a whore.

*(**ANTHONY** exits. A moment and then **MARIE** enters.)*

EDWARD. Where's Mark?

MARIE. Apologizing to Anthony. That didn't go very well.

EDWARD. No.

MARIE. Maybe because it was the first time. It's terrible about the swimming pool.

EDWARD. Yes it is. The swimming pool was meant to be a good thing.

MARIE. It is a good thing. And we'll get it refilled and we'll start again.

*(**MARK** enters.)*

MARK. I'm sorry, I don't like him.

EDWARD. You didn't see his best side.

MARK. What is his best side?

EDWARD. He's very bright. And he's ambitious.

MARK. He hates women. That's not very bright.

EDWARD. It's a different culture here.

MARK. Some cultural differences aren't acceptable. Not when they're based on ignorance and prejudice.

EDWARD. That's universal.

MARK. That doesn't make it alright! My god, they're all killing each other! "I don't use condoms…"

MARIE. That's the church.

MARK. They should have taken our church and told us to shove it!

EDWARD. I agree. But they didn't.

MARIE. I'd really be very interested to meet his wife. Do you think we could have them both round, Edward?

MARK. You two just love to socialize, don't you? What the hell do you think you and his wife are going to talk about, Marie?

MARIE. I don't know. That's precisely why I'd like to meet her.

EDWARD. Apparently his wife has AIDS. He just told me.

MARIE. She just had a baby.

MARK. Why doesn't he... You know he sees prostitutes? He probably gave it to her.

EDWARD. He doesn't see prostitutes.

MARK. How do you know? He offered to take me to one. He had a look on his face... I want to go home.

EDWARD. Are we going to eat?

MARIE. *(To* MARK*)* Well you're going tomorrow.

EDWARD. *(To* MARIE*)* We'll be back to see him soon.

MARIE. Does anybody mind if I work for a while?

EDWARD. Don't you want to taste the chicken?

MARIE. No!

MARK. I'm not hungry either.

MARIE. I'll be down later.

(MARIE *exits.*)

MARK. It's my last night. You'd think she might want to spend some time together.

EDWARD. She said she'd be down later. She was writing every night before you got here. I've never seen her work like this. It's good. She was blocked for a long time in New York.

MARK. She sent me some things from New York. I thought they were good.

EDWARD. They were good. But she was struggling.

MARK. You help her a lot.

EDWARD. Other people have always helped poets.

MARK. I don't think she should chew those sticks.

EDWARD. She's always liked drugs. Mild drugs. It's very common here. It's like alcohol. She drank in Germany, she smoked pot in New York, and now she's chewing Khat in Africa. That's Marie.

MARK. I don't want to visit here again, Edward. Have you any idea how long you're going to be staying?

EDWARD. I'll be out here at least another year. Marie is free to do whatever she wants. I don't hold her here, Mark. I get the distinct impression that you feel I do, but I don't, I assure you.

MARK. Well good, I'll report that to the family.

EDWARD. I didn't realize you'd be giving a report.

MARK. We worry about her.

EDWARD. Mark. She's fine. She's happy.

MARK. Of course she's happy here. She's a depressive. They feed off misery.

EDWARD. One depression. In her twenties. It's normal.

MARK. She's not a stable person.

EDWARD. She doesn't seem unstable to me at all.

MARK. You don't know her like I do.

EDWARD. I've known her as long as you have.

MARK. I'm her brother. Who are you?

EDWARD. In a way I'm her brother too.

MARK. She –

EDWARD. Mark. You've got a new family now. Leave me to mine. Listen, I was thinking of trying to get the people round here interested in bio-gas.

MARK. Oh.

EDWARD. I've always thought that bio-gas is underestimated. We did a class about it at school once. It always sounded very practical to me. Do you know that it could create a third of the energy we get from coal?

MARK. It leaves a lot of waste.

EDWARD. So does nuclear power.

MARK. I know. The thing is, there is no solution.

EDWARD. Come on, Mark. There is a best option. Do you think we could get bio-gas off the ground here? Is that something you might be interested in helping us with?

MARK. I live in London.

EDWARD. We have email.

MARK. I could send you some literature if you'd like.

EDWARD. That would be wonderful. I just want to get people talking, you know? About what can be done. To show that there are still possibilities. It's like the swimming pool. I know it's nothing. But it gives people hope, you see. And that's important.

MARK. Hope in what?

EDWARD. Hope that there are alternatives. Hope that happiness is accessible. That this is a country, or a village, where there can be a swimming pool. And people can...

MARK. Frolic?

EDWARD. Sure, why not? Why shouldn't they? Let them frolic, for how ever long.

MARK. Not long now.

EDWARD. There'll be other people, Mark. They'll always be more people. And some might get out. Like Anthony. He's got great spirit. *(A beat.)* I'm sorry that what you've seen has shocked you, Mark. But isn't it better to have seen it? You'll wake up in London with your new wife one morning and you'll know what's happening on the other side of the world.

MARK. I already knew.

EDWARD. But you didn't feel this way in London. So sad. You've learned something more. Isn't that useful?

MARK. I don't know if it's useful. Before it was abstract. I blamed the church, I blamed the colonialists, I blamed the governments. Now I blame you. You're enjoying it, Edward.

(MARK exits.)

ACT III

*(It is late afternoon, a few weeks later. The boxes are gone and now there's a rug. It is raining outside, and has been for several weeks. **EDWARD** is sitting with a drink, writing on a notepad. **MARIE** enters. She circles the room vaguely. **EDWARD** looks up, then returns to his work.)*

EDWARD. How's it going up there?

MARIE. I don't know... It's getting very long. I'm worried. It's not... People don't like long poems anymore. What are you working on?

EDWARD. An article.

MARIE. Another article?

EDWARD. It's for *The New York Times*. Bringing art to the people. That kind of thing. It might attract the gallery more funding.

MARIE. You've got enough funding.

EDWARD. You can't have too much. What do you think of this? "It is a commonplace about art that it is supposed to uplift. Here, such inspiration is sorely needed for a people currently blighted by such socio-economic hardship. The gallery, not yet complete, is already causing tremendous excitement among locals, generating a sense of hope, not simply in the future, but in the interest the West is taking in their plight by devoting money, time and energy to this ambitious project."

MARIE. That's good. It's not true, though, is it?

EDWARD. People are excited.

MARIE. Really?

EDWARD. Some people. And wait till it opens. Imagine, imagine what it's going to mean to these people to be able to go in, for free, and look at a Rothko. And we've got some Van Goghs. One definitely, we might

41

get another one, I'm working on it. And there's going to be local art. I've already seen two transparencies of paintings that are coming in from Zimbabwe.

MARIE. That's hardly local.

EDWARD. I met an artist from the city a few weeks ago. The plumber brought him in, and showed me his work. I'm definitely going to try and use it. It's wonderful.

MARIE. What is it?

EDWARD. He makes bowls. Wooden bowls. They're quite beautiful. I was going to ask you if we should get one.

MARIE. A bowl?

EDWARD. Yes, I thought we could use it for fruit. They're not expensive.

MARIE. You can't leave fruit out in a bowl here. You have to eat it immediately. Otherwise the flies come.

EDWARD. We could just have one on display.

MARIE. Form but no function.

EDWARD. Its function would be to be beautiful.

MARIE. An empty bowl. Yes, I suppose it would be rather poignant. We can get one if you'd like.

EDWARD. The flies have gone anyway now. With the rain.

MARIE. I wish the rain would stop.

EDWARD. Apparently it doesn't stop. Not for months. I don't know how much of the gallery we're supposed to get done with the weather like this. And four men were off last month anyway.

MARIE. I feel… very heavy.

EDWARD. I hope you're not getting ill. Although Michael Lee did say there was a very good doctor in the city. We could ask him about it next week.

MARIE. It's so strange he's staying with us. We don't know him.

EDWARD. He's not staying long. He just wants to pick up a few things. It is his house. I didn't know what else to say.

MARIE. Why did he leave?

EDWARD. The bank closed down their branch last year. He and his wife went back to Boston. He sounds nice.

MARIE. Everyone's getting out.

EDWARD. Not everyone. We're getting in a lot of contemporary art from New York. And a few pieces from Germany.

MARIE. Oh great. What did you get? Sculptures made of toothpaste? Five canvasses all painted red? Don't tell me, the artists' urine in different shaped bottles, labeled with what he'd drunk that day.

EDWARD. The toothpaste sculpture is quite an important piece. Actually.

MARIE. Sorry.

EDWARD. I did get it for the gallery. It's a coup, I thought.

MARIE. How much did you pay for it?

EDWARD. We're getting everything cheap. It looks good on the artists' resumes to have pieces hung abroad.

MARIE. How much?

EDWARD. Why do you want to know?

MARIE. Because I think a sculpture made of toothpaste is a stupid idea.

EDWARD. It's original.

MARIE. I think there's a reason it hasn't been done before. All good stories have been told at least a thousand times before.

EDWARD. Yes, what you do is so much more important than what I do.

(Pause.)

MARIE. Edward. I don't feel well.

EDWARD. Should I call that doctor?

MARIE. No, I… I feel like I'm changing. And I don't feel in control of it particularly.

EDWARD. But it's not like before?

MARIE. I'm getting up, aren't I? I get up, I shower, I walk about the house, I write. I just feel… heavy. It's probably just the rain.

EDWARD. It's hard for you staying home all day.

MARIE. Yes. And now Nsugo gone. There's no one to talk to. Can we ask her to come back? Just to clean?

EDWARD. She needs to be with her children.

MARIE. Says who?

EDWARD. We both did. I gave her some money. I give Anthony money, I give Nsugo money, at least the rug was cheap. I don't feel very well, either. I think it is the weather. It must be.

MARIE. If there's going to be so much press I think we should tell them what's going on here.

EDWARD. Everybody knows, Marie. There's just not anything anyone can do. We just have to wait. This will pass. And there will be new life here. That's what this article is. That's what I'm saying. New people will come.

MARIE. Yes. Yes of course how silly of me.

EDWARD. What's silly of you?

MARIE. To forget. That life is cheap.

EDWARD. After here, I was thinking Paris. I've been offered some consultancy. It's an open offer. We could go whenever we want. Next year. The year after. Paris is good for writers. We wouldn't have to stay in the city if we didn't want to. There are some beautiful parts of France. Parts that have barely changed since the twelfth century.

MARIE. Paris is for lovers.

(Pause.)

(Without emotion) I have to say…

I do want to make love, Edward…

I need to.

(EDWARD *looks down at his article.)*

EDWARD. Maybe you'll meet someone when we have the opening. Can you hang on for a couple of months?

(Pause.)

MARIE. What's wrong with us? Here we are in the middle of

Africa in this big house, with these walls of paintings, and our books Edward, the books we've put together on the shelves... Oh God! What are we doing?

EDWARD. We're happy aren't we?

MARIE. Are we?

EDWARD. I am. I thought you were too. Do you really want to risk everything we have? For sex?

MARIE. You're going to leave me eventually.

EDWARD. Don't be ridiculous. You're the one who might run off and leave me!

MARIE. Well neither of us can go anywhere here.

(A beat.)

It really is funny to think there are places in France where you sit all day long at a little table outside a little café, waiting to be served the good red wine and thinking how beautiful it all is. How peaceful.

(Loud knocking.)

EDWARD. Who's that?

MARIE. Shall I answer?

EDWARD. Who would visit?

*(A moment, then **MARIE** exits and returns with **ANTHONY**.)*

ANTHONY. I need to talk to you, Edward!

EDWARD. You're soaking.

ANTHONY. There is much rain.

EDWARD. Do you want a drink?

ANTHONY. I need to talk to you.

EDWARD. Alright...

ANTHONY. In private. Please.

*(A brief pause. **MARIE** exits.)*

EDWARD. What is it?

ANTHONY. I have seen a doctor. I am well.

EDWARD. Good. *(Remembering)* Good!

ANTHONY. A good doctor. In the city. I do not have the disease. I checked. I was scared after that night, Edward. I went to this doctor. Here is the report.

(He hands a sodden document to EDWARD.*)*

The doctor says I am lucky. He tells me many people will die. It is like you said. You get it from the blood.

*(*EDWARD *hands the paper back to Anthony.)*

My wife, she will die. And the child. He is sure.

EDWARD. I'm so sorry, Anthony.

ANTHONY. My wife, she says I must come to you.

EDWARD. Anthony, I can't… What?

ANTHONY. My wife says it's okay for me to leave. She will stay here alone. It is best. She says. She says it, Edward!

EDWARD. Anthony, I said I would investigate.

ANTHONY. Then investigate!

EDWARD. We still have the gallery. I'm not leaving.

ANTHONY. But when you do, you will take me with you?

EDWARD. You're just going to leave your wife to die here? Alone?

ANTHONY. You, you live in this big house. You don't understand how it is for me. How it is for everyone. Where I live… you do not know, Edward, what I come from every day when I come to the gallery. Everyone where I live is dying! There is silence everywhere while people wait for their death to come for them. No one speaks about it, we just walk through it, we are stepping over bodies to walk to the road. No one is clearing the bodies, Edward. There are people lying outside their house, you don't know if they sleep or if they are dead now.

EDWARD. This is in our village?

ANTHONY. There is a smell and there is nowhere in the village you can go that does not have that smell. Some people think you can catch it just from the smell. I think that too, sometimes, at night. But I do not understand why I think that because the smell is sweet.

EDWARD. Where in the village?

ANTHONY. Step off the road and walk down the hill and you would see Africa. There are hundreds of families. With no running water, no proper doors, or windows, or beds, Edward, or chairs like these! It is nothing! Nothing! You would refuse to live this way. I refuse it too, Edward.

EDWARD. Anthony. There are people who are working on a cure.

ANTHONY. The doctor said it is too late.

EDWARD. Not for everybody.

ANTHONY. Yes, for everybody here. This is Africa! We must build a gallery somewhere else, where people are alive and they can come to see your pictures. Why don't you go back to America?

EDWARD. I'm here. I'm building a gallery.

ANTHONY. You know the other friends of mine who are working with us? Nick? Steve? They have a foam in their mouths. When they are talking you can see the white. They will not come back to work, after the rains.

EDWARD. You'll have to find people to replace them. This week.

ANTHONY. Everyone is sick! Everyone I know is sick! There is no one to work! But I can still work. We should work somewhere else.

EDWARD. Anthony, it's not as simple… I can't just telephone someone –

ANTHONY. You can! You said you can! You said you know many people. Did you send a photograph to anyone, Edward? It was expensive. To make the photographs. It was expensive to see this doctor.

EDWARD. I will send the photographs. I promise. I'll do it tomorrow.

ANTHONY. You promise me, you promise me, you promise me these things. I cannot make you keep your promises.

EDWARD. Look, I have to work now, Anthony. Would you like to borrow something? For the rain?

ANTHONY. No.

(He starts to exit.)

EDWARD. Is there anything we can do? For your wife?

ANTHONY. I have asked you to help me.

*(**ANTHONY** exits. A pause.)*

EDWARD. Marie! Marie!

*(**MARIE** enters from the upstairs.)*

Marie!

MARIE. What? I'm working now.

EDWARD. Anthony says – It's a lot of people who are ill. I'm worried.

MARIE. You're worried about what? The people?

EDWARD. That this might have been a mistake. I need to call London.

MARIE. And say what?

EDWARD. The sponsors have a right to know exactly what the situation is.

MARIE. Everyone does know. It's in the papers.

EDWARD. No, not the way he described it. He said the dead just lie outside their houses. That no one will clear them. That there's a village near here –

MARIE. We know the village –

EDWARD. Not that village! Another village! Off the road!

MARIE. Where off the road?

EDWARD. I don't know! Off the road! Walk down the hill! That's where everyone is! Dying! It's a twenty minute walk! Everyone said we were crazy to come in the first place.

MARIE. That's not true. Some people were ever so excited for us, going all the way to Africa.

EDWARD. You know, if this is a doomed project it's better to accept that now than spend more money.

MARIE. So you'd just leave? Just leave them here? What about their jobs?

EDWARD. The men are too sick to build the gallery!

MARIE. You said there were always more people!

EDWARD. There's that job in Paris. What about Paris?

MARIE. That's not what we talked about.

EDWARD. If you'd heard him.

MARIE. I didn't need to hear him. I knew! This isn't new information!

EDWARD. It is to me! It was the way that he put it.

MARIE. Oh... You didn't understand before... I don't want to leave. We said we'd be here at least a year. We agreed. I'm writing. I can't just move.

EDWARD. We might have to. I'm calling the sponsors.

MARIE. Don't call them.

EDWARD. They have a right to know.

MARIE. A sense of hope, remember? You said you were doing it to give a sense of hope.

EDWARD. Look at what happened with the swimming pool. In less than a week they had to drain it.

MARIE. The interest the West is taking, you said. Devoting time, money and energy. So we're just going to leave? It's too difficult?

EDWARD. What do you want me to do! I can't solve this!

MARIE. I want you to stay!

EDWARD. What, and watch? I don't want to!

MARIE. But I do!

EDWARD. You want us to stay and watch? Soon we'll be the only ones here!

MARIE. We should watch Edward. And care! And not just turn away because it frightens you!

EDWARD. We're not staying here.

MARIE. Aren't we?

EDWARD. No.

MARIE. You mean you're not staying here.

EDWARD. You are?

MARIE. Yes.

EDWARD. Who's going to pay for the house?

(A beat.)

MARIE. Don't you dare think I can't manage without you, Edward. I can.

*(**MARIE** gets her coat.)*

EDWARD. What are you doing?
For god's sake, Marie. It's getting late. It's pouring with rain. You can't –

MARIE. I'm sick of this house. I'm sick of staying in this house, all day, everyday, doing nothing!

EDWARD. So let's leave!

MARIE. I'm not just going to leave, Edward!

EDWARD. What, you'll stay here without me?

MARIE. Yes, yes why not? We're not lovers. We don't have to be together. It's a convenience, isn't it?

EDWARD. You've been chewing that stuff. I can see. Your eyes look funny. Just sit down. Please. Just sit down for a moment.

MARIE. You never chose me. For you're very own. So I don't sit when you tell me to sit. I don't sit when someone we know is dying in the middle of Africa!

EDWARD. Who the hell do we know?

MARIE. We know Nsugo! I liked her. My God, Edward, I'm not going to sit!

*(**MARIE** exits.)*

ACT IV

(It is late afternoon, a week later. It is still raining. MICHAEL LEE *has just arrived. He is surveying the room.)*

MICHAEL. I like what you've done with the place.

EDWARD. Good.

MICHAEL. All the pictures. Very nice. I don't go in for the modern stuff myself so much. I like the pre-Raphaelites. My wife was on me to get an original. You can still get them, you know. But they're expensive. Good investment though, right?

EDWARD. Can be. Absolutely.

MICHAEL. How much are these worth? Out of curiosity?

EDWARD. Which?

MICHAEL. That one. What did you pay for that?

EDWARD. That's worth about eight thousand dollars.

MICHAEL. You're kidding me.

(He takes a closer look.)

MICHAEL. It's just newspaper print, right?

EDWARD. You're paying for the artist, really. This guy's doing very well at the moment.

MICHAEL. I guess he is if he can cut up a newspaper and people are paying eight thousand dollars for it.

EDWARD. It's increased in value since I bought it.

MICHAEL. No kidding...

EDWARD. I've been following him since he was young.

MICHAEL. *(Examining the picture)* What's it say here? I can't see without my glasses.

EDWARD. It's not really about the words.

MICHAEL. Oh boy. Some old lady in New Jersey poisoned her grandchild. There's no date. So people pay a lot of money for this kind of thing, huh? I like a painting. No one does a nice painting any more. Why is that?

51

EDWARD. Some do. If you're interested I could show you some contemporary painting when I get back to New York.

MICHAEL. Sure. Sure. You know why I like the pre-Raphaelites? All that hair. Women never have hair like that any more. Why is that?

EDWARD. I'm not sure.

MICHAEL. Do you smell something?

EDWARD. No.

MICHAEL. There's a funny smell. You know what I used to have hanging in this room? A zebra skin. Jean hated it. That really stank. I'd spray it, but I couldn't get rid of the stink.

EDWARD. Can I get you anything? Some tea?

MICHAEL. I'll have a scotch.

EDWARD. I'm afraid we don't have any.

MICHAEL. I bought you a bottle on the plane.

EDWARD. Thank you.

(*Michael nods to a plastic bag and* EDWARD *takes a bottle from it and pours himself and* MICHAEL LEE *a drink.*)

MICHAEL. So you're moving back to New York, huh?

EDWARD. Next week.

MICHAEL. The gallery didn't work out?

EDWARD. No. There's a lot of sickness in the village. It's a bad time.

MICHAEL. I heard.

EDWARD. Although we haven't made an official announcement so I'd be grateful if you didn't say anything at the moment. I'm sorry we're leaving the house sooner than we said.

MICHAEL. No problem. Found a buyer.

EDWARD. Really?

MICHAEL. Company from Washington. Didn't tell me much. They make paper.

EDWARD. When do they come?

MICHAEL. In a few weeks. They want to use it as a base, is all they said. So I'm selling and I'm out of here. It's worked out fine.

EDWARD. I'm glad.

MICHAEL. Jean always said I was crazy to buy this place anyway, but I fell in love with it. Everyone else from the bank lived in the city. But I didn't mind the drive. I liked the idea of being somewhere remote. You been hunting yet?

EDWARD. No, no I haven't.

MICHAEL. You should do that before you leave. You can pay a guide. It's a lot of fun. I got a lion, once.

EDWARD. Really?

MICHAEL. You're not supposed to hit the lions. But I saw it and I shot it. Didn't even think about it. Instinct. And a lion would eat you soon as look at you, so I didn't lose any sleep over it.

EDWARD. Who lived in this house before you did?

MICHAEL. Bought it from an old British lady. Broke her heart to sell it to me. I guess her family had been here for generations. But most of the other British moved from here years ago anyway, and her daughter persuaded her to move back to England. Or Scotland. I forget. Have you been happy here?

EDWARD. Yes, I have.

MICHAEL. Best years of my life, in some ways. But Jean hated it here. Got bored. Nothing for her to do. She works back in the States so she was glad to leave. And the country will drive you crazy after a few years anyway. It was time to go.

EDWARD. How does it drive you crazy?

MICHAEL. I was on a train once, my wife wanted to take a train, don't ask me why. And it stops in the middle of nowhere, so I ask a guy why, and he told me it's because the driver had gone to take a leak. And I said, "Is he planning on coming back any time soon," because we hadn't moved for about twenty minutes, and he said, "Relax man. This is Africa." Half the time that train moved so slowly you could walk next to it. But the country's beautiful. I'll give them that. Beautiful scenery. And the wildlife. Oh boy. You know you can hand-feed giraffes somewhere around here?

EDWARD. Yes, we've been.

MICHAEL. You can bet when the British were here the trains ran on time.

EDWARD. Well, we built the railway.

MICHAEL. Exactly.Everyone's always attacking the West. We shouldn't be here, we shouldn't be there. But in reality, everyone uses the god damn railroad. Everyone's always complaining about America. But my god, when the British had power, they used it too.

EDWARD. Yes they did.

MICHAEL. What are you gonna do? Progress corrupts. *(A beat.)* The British did some pretty terrible things in Africa, didn't they?

EDWARD. Yes.

MICHAEL. Why did you cut off all those people's hands in the Congo?

EDWARD. That was the Belgians.

MICHAEL. It's a good time to leave. This country's in the toilet. Even driving here from the airport, I was shocked. Everything's closed. There used to be a restaurant in town where you could eat zebra. Is that gone?

EDWARD. I haven't seen it.

MICHAEL. Pity. You could eat anything. Zebra, impala, the impala was good… Warthog. Over two years I tried everything on the menu. Except turtle. Couldn't bring myself to eat turtle. You know what I mean? I kept thinking about their little heads.

EDWARD. I do find it rather difficult not to feel guilty about leaving. Just leaving so abruptly. Leaving everyone behind. Did you find that?

MICHAEL. What are you supposed to do? Take them with you?

EDWARD. No, no of course not.

Do you remember Anthony?

MICHAEL. Oh yes.

EDWARD. He wants me to help him.

MICHAEL. He was the same with me. I said to him once,

"why do you want to move to America? Look to Africa. Stay and rebuild it." I tried to inspire him, you know?

EDWARD. There's not a tremendous amount of work for him here. Especially now I'm leaving.

MICHAEL. There's no work in the States. It's a terrible time.

EDWARD. I know. I tried to explain to him.

MICHAEL. Edward. Guess what? You're not the bank.

EDWARD. No.

MICHAEL. You've had some success. Good for you. It does not mean you owe the world.

EDWARD. I know.

MICHAEL. Do the right thing. Give to charity. Sit on some boards. But don't let everyone that comes along bleed you dry. Take it from me. Or after every conversation you have, you realize you've been robbed.

EDWARD. I made some calls for Anthony. Nobody's very interested.

MICHAEL. I know. I did the same. I made a few calls but it didn't work out. Immigration's tight.

EDWARD. Sure.

MICHAEL. Everyone's got problems of their own.

EDWARD. I freelance. I don't have a company to put him in or anything.

MICHAEL. You came here, you employed him, now it's over.

(He finishes his drink.)

Are you putting me in the back bedroom?

EDWARD. No. No, I thought the one next door. You see, Nsugo is staying with us at the moment.

MICHAEL. You had her move in?

EDWARD. She and her children are staying here for a while.

MICHAEL. The kids are staying here? All four.

EDWARD. No, just two. I hope that's alright.

MICHAEL. You're renting the place. If that's what you want to do...

EDWARD. Marie took them in – Oh, there she is.

*(The two men rise as **MARIE** enters from upstairs.)*

MARIE. The children are asleep.

EDWARD. Marie, this is Michael Lee. Michael, this is Marie.

MICHAEL. How do you do?

MARIE. Well. I am well.

MICHAEL. Is Nsugo coming down? I brought her something.

MARIE. She's singing to the children. I can't make her stop.

MICHAEL. I'll go up and say hello.

MARIE. She says they'll be dead by morning. I don't think they will. They seem a little better, to me. I don't know. I'm not a doctor. But there's no point in them seeing a doctor now, she says. I agree with her. They're not going to get well.

MICHAEL. What's wrong with them?

MARIE. There's a boy and a girl. She's eight and he's nine.

EDWARD. Unfortunately, the children, Nsugo's children, have AIDS. Marie found them in the village. And their living circumstances were less than... so she brought them here.

MARIE. Does any one want any soup? I'm going to cook some soup, I think. Nsugo and I chopped up some vegetables this morning.

(*To* **MICHAEL**)

I've been learning to cook. I couldn't cook at all before I came here.

EDWARD. We've been eating a lot of soup.

MARIE. Yes, that's all I can do at the moment. But with soup you get so much. So many different vitamins. And it's easy to swallow. Especially for the children. They have a foam in their mouth. It's... what's the word?

EDWARD. Michael said he ate on the plane.

MARIE. Candida. I'll make a big pot.

(**MARIE** *exits.*)

EDWARD. I am sorry about this. When she found them, the children were so sick you see, and Marie and Nsugo had become close, she couldn't bring herself to leave them there.

MICHAEL. Yes, I see. It's admirable. So they're next door to me?

EDWARD. Yes. I hope they won't disturb you. They... there is an element of crying.

MICHAEL. Are you going crazy?

EDWARD. Well it's not easy. Marie brought them in. What could I say?

MICHAEL. I always told Jean, you don't let it go too far. Nothing against the Africans. But we're talking about different worlds. You don't want to confuse the two. Let them see how we live and they'll resent it. And who can blame them? But that's the way it is, so best to keep it all separate.

EDWARD. Yes. I'm not really sure what to do.

MICHAEL. You're leaving soon. When?

EDWARD. At the end of next week.

MICHAEL. So. There you go.

EDWARD. The thing is... Marie says she doesn't want to come with.

MICHAEL. She wants to stay here by herself?

EDWARD. She feels very attached to Nsugo and the children.

MICHAEL. What about you?

EDWARD. It's a complicated situation.

MICHAEL. Where would she stay? Does she know I'm selling the house?

EDWARD. I'll tell her.

MICHAEL. It will pass. She's emotional. It's understandable. But she isn't going to stay here if she doesn't have anywhere to live.

EDWARD. I have to say, she's not been herself recently. At all. Obviously I can't just leave her here. I'm responsible.

MICHAEL. Of course. What does she do again?

EDWARD. She's a poet. She's quite widely published.

MICHAEL. So she's a little flaky.

EDWARD. Yes. A little. It's very stressful here, that's all. It's getting to her. To both of us. I am worried about her. There was one time, a long time ago, in London... She suffered a very serious depression. She wasn't in her right mind, exactly. For a brief period. Six months or so. It's extremely common with artists.

MICHAEL. Oh sure.

EDWARD. I worry…

MICHAEL. Have you taken her to see a doctor?

EDWARD. I was actually hoping that you could recommend one. Although I've mentioned the idea a few times to her and she doesn't want to see anyone.

MICHAEL. What about her family?

EDWARD. I don't want to worry them. I just need to get her on the plane.

(**MARIE** *enters.*)

MARIE. I've put it on a low light.

(*She sits.*)

Have you noticed the lizards?

EDWARD. I saw a few this morning.

MARIE. There's more than a few. Nsugo says the lizards mean death.

EDWARD. Really?

MARIE. Oh yes. It's an old legend. God asked man if he wanted to be reincarnated after he died. Man decided yes. They sent a lizard with the answer to god. But the lizard was a vain lizard. He walked slowly so everyone would notice that his skin glittered in sunlight. So of course the lizard was overtaken by an evil hare. The hare ran up to God and said: I was sent by man, they do not want be reincarnated. God made it so. And when the lizard did finally get there, it was all too late.And ever since then the lizard has been bad luck. The San people say anyway. There are lizards everywhere I'm noticing.

MICHAEL. Edward was telling me you're a writer. You must like these old stories.

MARIE. I particularly like this one.

MICHAEL. Are you working on anything at the moment?

MARIE. Yes.

EDWARD. Every time I try to talk to her she's writing.

MICHAEL. Poems?

MARIE. One poem.

MICHAEL. What kind of poetry do you write?

MARIE. What kind?

MICHAEL. Does it rhyme?

EDWARD. Sometimes. Sometimes it rhymes, doesn't it? Are you ready to go and get this one published?

MARIE. Edward, it's a long poem – no one's going to publish it. It's pages and pages.

EDWARD. Maybe this one will be the book.

MARIE. Yes, maybe. I think maybe it's the best thing I've written.

EDWARD. I'd like to see.

MARIE. It pours out of me. All day.

MICHAEL. Sounds like maybe you should take a break kid.

MARIE. I do sleep. But there are the children. We have to keep washing the sheets. We keep running out of them because the children can't control their bowels any more. So I wash them. And then their little bodies. They hardly notice the shower though. I thought they'd be so excited.

MICHAEL. If they're that sick we should take them to a hospital.

MARIE. Should we? There are hundreds more. I don't think there's room for all of them. And these two are peaceful here.

MICHAEL. Edward tells me you plan to stay after he leaves.

MARIE. Yes. I think that's best. There's so much to do.

MICHAEL. You realize of course that I have to give the house to somebody else.

MARIE. Who?

MICHAEL. Some men.

MARIE. Some white men?

MICHAEL. Yes. White men.

MARIE. Yes, they will come I suppose. There's going to be so much space, they wouldn't let it go to waste, would they?

EDWARD. So we can't keep the house, you see?

MARIE. I can go back to the village. With Nsugo. But I wish you'd let us stay here, Mr. Lee.

MICHAEL. You can call me Michael.

MARIE. I wish you would. There's running water here, that's a help. And we can cook easily. I thought we could turn the place into a sort of hospice. That would be more useful than a swimming pool. Nsugo was telling me that the people think the swimming pool cursed the village.

EDWARD. Why do they think that? This was all going on before the swimming pool.

MARIE. Because it's so drained and hopeless.

MICHAEL. What's this?

EDWARD. I built them a swimming pool.

MARIE. You mustn't let it upset you. You misunderstood what can be done. But now it's clear.

EDWARD. Oh really? Thank god. What are we supposed to do? I've been wondering.

MARIE. We must bear witness. We can't give very much. Acknowledgment. Regret. Admit our fault.

EDWARD. How is this our fault?

MARIE. I do not know your fault.

(To **MICHAEL***)*

Or yours. I will tell you mine. When I was eighteen I was driving in a car with Mark.

(To **MICHAEL***)*

Mark is my brother. And a black man, our age, was in the road, in the way of the car, so we had to slow down. And Mark said "naff off, nigger." And we both burst out laughing. And I don't know why.

(A beat.)

MICHAEL. I have a friend here, not near here, but a few hours drive away, who I thought we might have dinner with while I'm visiting. He's an American, a doctor. Lived here for twenty years.

EDWARD. That sounds like fun. What do you think?

MARIE. Would you like me to see a doctor, Edward?

EDWARD. Yes. I'm worried about you. You're scaring me.

MARIE. There's nothing to be frightened of, Edward. Nothing at all. It's time for us to separate. That's all. Do you understand? I can't go where you're going. It's become imaginary to me, do you see? I couldn't live there. And I don't think I could live with you.

EDWARD. You can't stay here by yourself.

MICHAEL. Marie, I really do think you should see a doctor. Edward tells me you've not been feeling well.

MARIE. Who are you?

MICHAEL. My name is Michael Lee.

MARIE. That isn't what I asked.

EDWARD. He wants to help us.

(*MARIE rises.*)

MARIE. You want to help? Then I beg you. Don't sell this house. Please.

(*She kneels in front of* **MICHAEL**.)

MICHAEL. Edward?

EDWARD. Marie. Stand up.

MARIE. Edward, do you remember when we got here there was screaming?

(*To* **MICHAEL**)

We heard it at night for the first few weeks. Nsugo told me later it was the women mourning. But they've stopped that now. No reincarnation. Soon it will be quiet. Let us stay until then.

MICHAEL. (*To* **EDWARD**) I'm taking my bags upstairs.

MARIE. You can't look at me can you?

MICHAEL. You know what I see when I look? A girl that's been here too long.

MARIE. Try and stay downstairs as much as you can. The children wake very easily. I'll take the bags.

(**MARIE** *gets up, and crosses to* **MICHAEL LEE**'*s bags. She picks them up and exits upstairs. A brief pause.*)

MICHAEL. Very emotional.

EDWARD. What do you think I should do?

MICHAEL. Take a look at what she's writing.

EDWARD. Why?

MICHAEL. You'll be able to tell, won't you? From that. I think she needs medical attention. For a start she needs something to calm her down. I'll call the doctor in the morning, see what he thinks.

EDWARD. I can't look at her work without her permission.

MICHAEL. She doesn't have to know. Edward, this is serious. You've got a week before leaving her here. I think we'd better find out.

EDWARD. Find out what?

MICHAEL. How far gone she is. Now don't worry. We'll get her out of here. Get her to the doctors in New York. She'll be right as rain in a few weeks.

EDWARD. Alright.

MICHAEL. Good.

EDWARD. Thank you, Michael.

MICHAEL. My pleasure.

(**NSUGO** *enters.*)

Nsugo. Michael Lee. Remember? Jean sends her best. She bought you something. Marie took it upstairs. It's a sweater.

NSUGO. Hello, Mr. Lee.

EDWARD. Do you need something?

NSUGO. Your woman needs soup, Edward. She is not eating enough.

EDWARD. Shall I get it?

NSUGO. I can get it. I thank you both. For letting us stay here. Also my children.

(*She exits into the other room.*)

MICHAEL. Does she know you're leaving?

EDWARD. I haven't said anything. I don't know if Marie has.

(**NSUGO** *re-appears with the bowl of soup and exits slowly up the stairs.*)

ACT V

(It is six in the evening, a few days later. The room is in boxes. **NSUGO** *and* **MARIE** *are sitting together, shelling peas.)*

MARIE. I don't understand why they're not back by now.

NSUGO. They have gone to the city.

MARIE. It's getting dark

NSUGO. Yes.

MARIE. How long can it take?

NSUGO. They have gone to the bank.

MARIE. Yes, with my work. Now why would they do that? *(A beat.)* I'll go and check on the children.

NSUGO. The children are sleeping.

MARIE. I'll put out the champagne glasses.

(She gets up and starts looking for them in open boxes.)

It doesn't matter if Anthony comes before they do. Then we can all be here toasting them as they come in. They'll get the shock of their lives.

(She finds the glasses, and begins unwrapping them, putting them out on the now empty drinks trolley.)

There was a party once, in Berlin, that Edward and I went to, and the bar was made of ice. And the barman would pour your drink down an ice funnel, and it would come out cold in your glass. It really was something. It really was. We used to go out a lot. We'd go to lots of places. We'd go and listen to music, or out to the theatre, or to eat, or parties. There were a lot of parties. And we'd go and we'd watch and laugh. At all the strange people.

NSUGO. You will miss Edward?

(A beat).

MARIE. I'll miss the idea of Edward. An earlier idea I had of him. Never mind. We can do without Edward.

NSUGO. Michael Lee told me this morning that I cannot stay here.

MARIE. No, we can stay here for two, maybe three weeks after they leave. After that I thought I could rent somewhere in the city. I have some money. I don't think anything costs very much. We can stay there with the children. And I can try and get a job. We both can.

NSUGO. There is no work.

MARIE. I'll find work.

NSUGO. I can go back to the village.

MARIE. There's really no need. I think we ought to keep the children somewhere clean if we can. They've been a lot better since they've been here. Remember? You thought they'd be dead by now. Some people are lucky. There are women, prostitutes, who should be dead. But they're not. They don't even have it. No one knows why. People are experimenting on them. *(A beat.)* You will come with me, won't you? I have some money. *(A beat.)* Nsugo, I want you to be my friend. Do you think we can be friends?

NSUGO. Sure.

MARIE. No, but real friends? Do you want to try to do that? Nsugo and Marie. They met in the big house in a village in Africa. Then they moved to town. What do you think?

NSUGO. I think one day you will go back.

MARIE. I'm not going back. Edward flies to New York tomorrow. I am not flying with him.

NSUGO. Why is this?

MARIE. In America, when I lived in America, it was very hard not to feel like the world was coming to an end, and the end would be caused by human error.

NSUGO. A country sees many things and lives through many times. This is one blink in God's eye.

MARIE. I can hear them.

*(A moment, then **EDWARD** and **MICHAEL LEE** enter from the outside.)*

EDWARD. At least it's stopped raining.

MICHAEL. Why won't they pave the damn roads here!

(They stop on seeing the two women.)

EDWARD. Hello.

(MARIE stands.)

MARIE. Give me my work.

(A beat. EDWARD hands her a sheaf of papers.)

You crept into my room, while I was asleep, and stole from me?

EDWARD. Yes.

(She exits. A moment. He exits after her.)

MICHAEL. These two… What are you gonna do? You making another soup?

NSUGO. Yes. Pea soup.

MICHAEL. What was that dish you made I liked so much?

NSUGO. Goat curry.

MICHAEL. That's right. Hardly any one eats goat in America. Did you know that? I don't know why.

NSUGO. Are there many goats?

MICHAEL. As many as anywhere else, I guess. Or we could get some. But no one wants to eat them.

NSUGO. The meat is tough. Cow is better.

MICHAEL. Yeah, we eat a lot of steak. How's Marie doing?

NSUGO. She is well.

MICHAEL. No, no she isn't. We took a look at Marie's poems. That she writes. Upstairs. You know her poems?

NSUGO. Yes.

MICHAEL. She expresses the desire in her writing to hurt other people. And does Edward get a beating! Oh boy. Edward the lizard. Edward's a lizard, and I'm a machine, apparently.

(EDWARD comes back in and makes himself a drink.)

EDWARD. She's furious.

MICHAEL. She'll get over it. I gotta tell you, Edward, I can't believe she's published.

EDWARD. Well she is.

MICHAEL. They're a downer. Who wants to read a downer?

EDWARD. That's the thing. She was always funny. Marie. Before. She was always very witty. Especially her writing. They never publish the other stuff.

NSUGO. Some is funny.

(A beat.)

EDWARD. She read it to you?

MICHAEL. We've just got to sit her down, tell her what the doctor said.

EDWARD. He didn't even meet her.

MICHAEL. He was pretty clear.

EDWARD. Because you kept pushing him. Because we paid him!

MICHAEL. She's your wife, Edward. If you want to give up on her and leave her here that's up to you. I wouldn't leave a member of my family here, not in a million years.

EDWARD. She's not actually my wife.

(A beat.)

MICHAEL. Oh. I assumed…

EDWARD. No. We're not family. We're not blood.

NSUGO. Family doesn't start with blood. That is time.

MICHAEL. But you two have been together for years, right?

EDWARD. Yes. Years.

MICHAEL. Okay.

(To **NSUGO***)*

Has she said anything to you?

NSUGO. She says she will not go. She has said that we will live together.

MICHAEL. Is that what you want? You want to live with a crazy white lady? She needs treatment.

NSUGO. What would the doctor do to her?

EDWARD. He'd talk to her. Make her feel better.

MICHAEL. Put her on pills.

NSUGO. She doesn't say to me that she feels bad.

EDWARD. You didn't know her before we came here. She was very different. She was always laughing, always making other people laugh. She was… Extraordinary.

MICHAEL. We have to make her understand that she can't just stay in the middle of Africa.

NSUGO. Why can't she stay here? I am staying here.

(A beat.)

MICHAEL. Marie needs to be with her family, Nsugo.

EDWARD. She's taking you to live in the city? She doesn't have much money, Nsugo. This is for you.

(He holds out a significant number of bills to **NSUGO** *and waits until she takes the money from him.)*

Thank you for everything you've done for us.

NSUGO. This is a lot of money.

EDWARD. It's really not that much for me. Please take it. You've worked for us, and I'm paying you. It's a bonus. This is the end of our time together. It's traditional.

NSUGO. With this money I can take the children.

EDWARD. Yes. Away from here. Where would you go?

NSUGO. To my family in Ghana.

EDWARD. Yes. Yes, Michael told me you had family there. Why are the champagne glasses out?

NSUGO. Anthony is coming to say goodbye.

*(**MARIE** enters from the upstairs.)*

EDWARD. Anthony is?

MARIE. I invited him to come and have a drink with us. He came over earlier. The poor thing went to the gallery site, now that the rain's stopped, I suppose he wanted to be there bright and early. And of course he arrived, and saw it all abandoned, and understandably he was quite confused because nobody told him, so he came over here. I explained the situation. I think he'd like to discuss it with you.

MICHAEL. Oh boy, that's going to be fun.

MARIE. I didn't mention that you were here, Michael. I thought it would be a nice surprise.

MICHAEL. Makes no difference to me. I'm going to finish packing. You still not coming with us?

MARIE. No, Nsugo and I are taking a house.

MICHAEL. Oh yeah? Good for you.

Nsugo, I've got a closet I need to empty in the kids' room.

MARIE. They're asleep.

MICHAEL. I need my things.

Oh, I know. I sicken you.

MARIE. Yes you do. You both do, actually.

MICHAEL. You should be thanking us. We're trying to help you.

MARIE. I don't need help.

MICHAEL. Oh yes you do, sweetheart. I read your work.

EDWARD. Michael –

MICHAEL. And you're one sick little puppy.

(A beat.)

EDWARD. It's very dark. You know it is.

MARIE. What did you expect it to be? Why do you think I didn't want to show you?

MICHAEL. We also showed it to a doctor.

MARIE. And what did he say?

MICHAEL. He said you're a danger to yourselfs, a danger to others, and we have to get you home.

MARIE. How am I a danger to others?

MICHAEL. Stab me with a knife? Is that what you want to do?

MARIE. Oh yes, I wrote that, didn't I? Only last night. I was just making some notes.

MICHAEL. They're potentially libelous, the things you wrote. Just so you know.

MARIE. You really took everything, didn't you. Right out of my desk. While I was sleeping. The subterfuge is amazing. Did the two of you wear night goggles?

MICHAEL. Nsugo, I need to get into that room.

*(He exits. **NSUGO** follows.)*

MARIE. We're all dangers to ourselves. Aren't we? And to others. Especially to others. Aren't we?

EDWARD. Marie?

I loved it. This poem.

(A beat.)

MARIE. No one will publish it, will they?

EDWARD. Come home. Make the rounds. Convince them.

MARIE. I'm too tired.

EDWARD. I gave Nsugo some money. She won't be staying here. She's got family in Ghana.

(Pause.)

MARIE. I'm still staying Edward.

EDWARD. What about me?

MARIE. What about you?

EDWARD. Aren't you going to miss me? I'm going to miss you. I don't want you to leave me.

MARIE. You're the one leaving, Edward.

EDWARD. We can't stay here! You'd have to be crazy to stay here.

MARIE. You know there is nothing more insulting than having your sanity questioned. Really nothing. So stop it. Because it frightens me.

EDWARD. You're behaving strangely!

MARIE. These are strange times. These are strange times, Edward! How do you expect me to behave? Don't you see? We're not equal, Edward, you and I. You're always the sane one and I the mad. You're rich, I'm poor. And you giving to me, giving to me, giving me a meal at a fancy, fancy restaurant… And both of us knowing how lucky I am to have you. To have your patronage. I don't want it any more. Stop patronizing me. I can't bear it.

EDWARD. You know what I can't bear? That once I had to sit by your bed and listen to you tell me that you didn't want to be alive any more. That I had to convince you that you should be. Mark couldn't do anything, your parents couldn't do anything, your friends couldn't do anything. I had to deal with it! And every day I know that I might wake up one morning, and you'll have forgotten what I told you and we'll have to start all over again. Are we starting all over again, Marie? Is that what this is? Because I don't know what to do!

MARIE. I'm sick of everyone thinking I need to be rescued! From myself! What do you think? That you swooped in out of the sky from Germany and suddenly everything was alright again? It was exhausting to pull myself out of that. You didn't do it, I did!

EDWARD. Oh and I had nothing to do with it? I took you back with me, gave you somewhere to live, cooked for you, looked after you –

MARIE. You were miserable there without me. Weren't you? And you've never once acknowledged it.

EDWARD. What if we got married? Would that help?

MARIE. Oh Edward. Not out of pity. Not out of fear. Just go home.

(Knocking.)

That's Anthony.

EDWARD. I don't know what to say to him. Why did you do this?

MARIE. Because you weren't even going to say goodbye!

*(She exits. She enters again with **ANTHONY**.)*

EDWARD. Anthony.

ANTHONY. *(To **EDWARD**)* Marie told me you were leaving.

EDWARD. Yes.

ANTHONY. I hear the gallery is closing, Edward. No work. You did not tell me. I went there this morning, now that the rains have stopped, I thought we would continue as normal. But nobody was there.

EDWARD. I'm sorry. The funders changed their minds. The economy is very difficult everywhere at the moment. Not just here.

ANTHONY. You didn't want to say goodbye?

EDWARD. I was going to say goodbye. It's been very busy. The decision was only made last week. Goodbye, Anthony.

ANTHONY. Can I have a drink? It is my birthday today, did Marie tell you?

EDWARD. No.

*(**MARIE** exits to get the champagne. The two men stand in silence until she comes back and pours them a drink.)*

Happy birthday.

ANTHONY. So. My wife died this week.

EDWARD. I'm sorry.

ANTHONY. Another woman is taking care of the child now. I am absolutely free to go with you.

EDWARD. I'm going alone, Anthony. I keep telling you.

ANTHONY. That is not what you told me before.

EDWARD. Yes it is, Anthony! I didn't promise anything!

ANTHONY. I thought we were friends. You would leave a friend here? I should have listened to the old people. You cannot be friends with the white man. They laughed at me. They have been laughing at me for a long time. Since Michael Lee.

EDWARD. This has nothing to do with being white.

ANTHONY. This has many things to do with being white. False promises, no care, here is some money, now I am taking the money away.

EDWARD. Look, you want to move to America, Anthony? Then find a way. Instead of sucking everybody else dry. I'm sorry. I can't help you any more.

ANTHONY. I don't believe you!

EDWARD. I've done a lot for you, Anthony. I gave you money.

ANTHONY. I worked for you.

EDWARD. More money than that! What did you do with it?

ANTHONY. I took my wife to a hotel in the city. This is where she died. I paid. She is still there. I left her in the room.

EDWARD. Alright, you want more money? Fine. I'll pay for your flight. How's that? You can fly to America.

(**EDWARD** *is searching for his wallet.*)

There's no work in America. You know that. You'll be as poor there as you are here. Worse maybe. And there's immigration… Just don't come to me. Please. I don't have any more cash. I'll write you a check. A thousand dollars. That will get you there. I'm writing you a check. Right now. That's all I'm doing. Then you're on your own.

ANTHONY. Why are you like this now, Edward? You were not like this before.

EDWARD. Because I'm sick of it! I'm sick of everyone thinking I know the answers!

(*He holds out the check.*)

Take the money.

ANTHONY. What can I do with a check of American dollars?

EDWARD. Take it.

ANTHONY. I have no way to make money from this piece of paper.

EDWARD. I don't have any cash!

ANTHONY. You would have to come with me to the bank in the city.

EDWARD. There's no time. We're leaving first thing in the morning.

MARIE. Edward!

EDWARD. What?

MARIE. That's not how you give charity.

ANTHONY. I saved your life, Edward.

> (**MICHAEL LEE** *enters with his luggage and stares at* **EDWARD** *waving the check in front of Anthony.*)

MICHAEL. *(To* **EDWARD***)* What are you doing?

EDWARD. Giving him money.

MICHAEL. *(To* **ANTHONY***)* I see you haven't changed.

ANTHONY. You came back…

MICHAEL. I leave in the morning.

> *(A beat.* **ANTHONY** *finishes his drink.)*

ANTHONY. Goodbye.

EDWARD. Goodbye, Anthony.

MARIE. Anthony.

ANTHONY. Yes?

MARIE. I am so sorry.

ANTHONY. My wife. She was not a whore. It was me. I gave it to her. It is my fault.

> *(He exits.)*

MICHAEL. I'm taking these to the car.

> *(We hear a shot.*
>
> *A moment.* **MICHAEL LEE** *exits. No one moves.* **MICHAEL** *returns.)*

MICHAEL. *(cont'd)* He's dead.

EDWARD. He can't be.

MICHAEL. He is. He used the shot gun. There's blood everywhere.

> *(**NSUGO** *runs in.)*

NSUGO. What has happened?

EDWARD. Anthony shot himself. He shot himself.

MICHAEL. Can you get some towels?

> *(**NSUGO** *and* **MARIE** *exit.)*
>
> You okay?

EDWARD. Am I okay?

MICHAEL. Coward's way out. That's all it is Edward. Not your fault. You were holding out a check for christsakes.

(NSUGO *passes through with towels.* MICHAEL LEE *follows.* EDWARD *is alone, holding his check.*

MICHAEL *comes back in. He is treading blood onto the floor.*)

MICHAEL. *(cont'd)* We can't leave him in the kitchen. Who the hell do you call about something like this? *(A beat.)* Does he have any family? We're going to have to bury him. Edward? We're going to have to bury him. I'll get a shovel.

EDWARD. The blood. The blood will attract the animals.

MICHAEL. We've got the gun.

(He exits. MARIE *enters. More blood on the floor.)*

MARIE. Edward? Edward.

*(EDWARD *stands there.)*

MARIE. *(Cont. Very gently)* Edward. Go inside.

*(EDWARD *exits.* MICHAEL LEE *passes through with a shovel.* NSUGO *enters.)*

MARIE. *(cont'd)* Is Edward crying?

NSUGO. Yes. Marie, I am going to Ghana.

MARIE. I know.

NSUGO. You will be here by yourself. I think you are my friend. A friend can remember, and say out there, across the sea is Nsugo. She was my friend in Africa. A friend does not have to stay in Africa too. A friend can tell what she has seen in her poems. People will remember this story.

MARIE. Yes.

NSUGO. I will remember also. Nsugo and Marie. They met in the big house in Africa. She tried to save her children. I am grateful.

*(EDWARD *enters.)*

EDWARD. Michael wants to bury him. What should I do?

MARIE. We're not burying him like an animal.

NSUGO. Many here are buried this way now.

MARIE. Edward?

(EDWARD exits.)

We'll buy him a coffin. That's something we can do, isn't it? Much cheaper than taking him to America.

(EDWARD enters.)

EDWARD. Michael's gone. He's spending the night at the airport.

MARIE. He's left everything behind. But you'll stay? For his funeral.

EDWARD. Of course.

MARIE. Anthony was a Christian.

EDWARD. We'll find a priest.

MARIE. They say suicides are damned.

EDWARD. I know.

MARIE. We won't tell them. And do we sit with the body, wash the body? That's what you do is it? I don't know...

EDWARD. I don't know...

MARIE. I think that's what you do. Sit with it all night. I think we should do that.

NSUGO. So I will make the soup.

(She exits with the peas.)

EDWARD. Is this my fault? Is it? Shall we stay here? I will.

MARIE. I don't know.

(She looks at him. He kisses her, clumsily. She lets him.)

EDWARD. We can go wherever you want. If you don't want to go back to America then what about Paris?

MARIE. Yes. Yes that's a place I suppose. Paris. We could try Paris.

(The lights start to fade. They sit holding on to each other. Two lost and frightened children.)

EDWARD. It's near London. And Mark's getting married in the spring.

End of Play

Printed in the United States
209438BV00005B/1-105/P